Making It! 👍

Cricketer

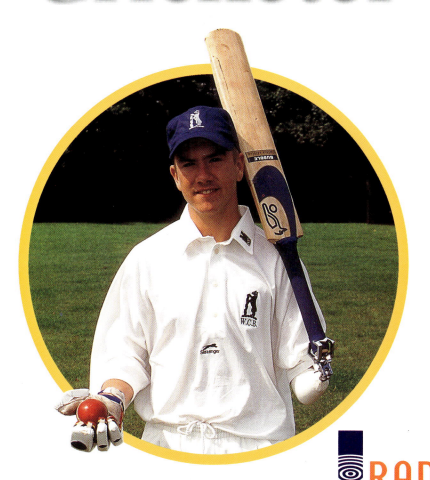

Eleanor Archer

W
FRANKLIN WATTS
NEW YORK • LONDON • SYDNEY

Dan is a cricketer. He plays for three different teams - the county team, the village team and a disability team.

Dan is physically disabled. A physical disability means that part of a person's body doesn't work fully.

Dan was born with one hand. People with physical disabilities find different ways of doing everyday things.

Dan is playing cricket for the disabled team on Sunday. He needs to be fit so today he visits his physiotherapist at the hospital.

A physiotherapist helps people to use all the muscles in their bodies properly.

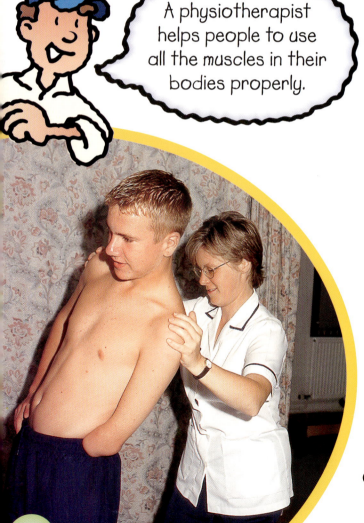

"Hello, Dan! How are you?" Nicki asks. Nicki checks the way Dan moves by making him do different stretches.

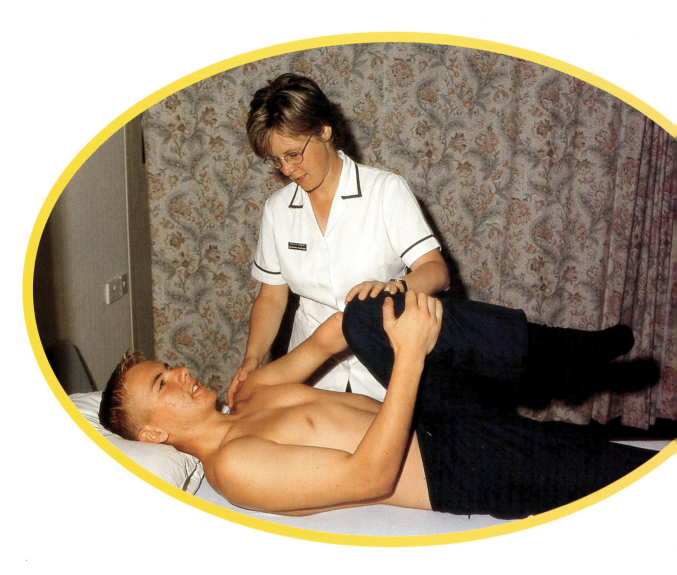

As he stretches, Dan tells Nicki about
the match. "If we win on Sunday we
go through to the final," he explains.
"Good luck, then!" says Nicki.

On Sunday, Dan gets up early to pack. He runs through the kit he needs. "Bat, helmet, pads..." he thinks to himself. There is a lot of safety equipment to take to the match.

"That's it!" Dan says as he puts his bag into the car.

When Dan and his mum arrive at the cricket ground, the manager is there to meet them.
"How's our best batsman?" he asks.
"Ready for action!"
laughs Dan.

Dan doesn't drive but he plans to take his test soon. He will get a car that is specially adapted for him.

Next Dan gets changed, ready for the match.
He puts on his pads. Cricketers wear an
all-white kit.

Dan has learned to do up his laces and buckles with one hand. Now he can do it very easily.

The team run around the pitch to warm up.

"One lap and then some leg stretches," the coach shouts.

It's important to warm up your muscles before exercising and then cool down afterwards.

When everyone has warmed
up, there's time to practise
bowling and batting
before the match.
"I feel nervous!"
Dan thinks as
he gets ready.

Dan has a
special arm
attachment
which allows
him to hold
the cricket
bat.

10

The team use the
nets to practise in.
Here they can
bat and bowl as
hard and as fast
as they like
because the ball
can't travel far.

Soon it's Dan's turn to practise batting.

"Yes!" shouts Dan as he hits the ball. "Six!" He gets six points if he hits the ball and it goes over the edge of the pitch without touching the ground.

At 2 p.m. the cricket match begins. Dan's team are fielding first. They have to stop the other team from getting any runs. "We need to get their batsmen out as quickly as possible," Dan says to his teammates.

There are many different ways in which someone can be physically disabled. Some of the team use wheelchairs to get around.

Dan is the team's first bowler. He bowls as fast as he can. He needs to hit the stumps behind the batsman to get the batsman out. "Not out!" calls the umpire.

Dan only wears his special arm attachment when he is batting. Some people have attachments to help them use computers, to draw or to paint.

Halfway through the match the teams stop for tea. "They're good," Dan says as he talks to his friends about the game.

After half an hour, it's time to start playing again. "It's our turn to bat now," Dan tells one of his team's supporters.

The batsmen take it in turns to bat. Dan waits for his turn with his teammates and some friends who have come to watch them.

Sometimes Dan wears a false arm. It looks just like his other arm. He often wears it when he goes out with his friends.

At last, it is Dan's turn.
The scores are close.
Dan needs to get twenty
runs for his team to win.

He hits the ball as
hard as he can.
"Six!" calls the umpire.

"Only another
fourteen to get,"
Dan thinks.
He concentrates
on the ball.

Dan plays well. He gets another six.
Then he hits the ball and gets two more runs.
Soon Dan has scored more runs than they need.
"That's it!" he shouts.

At the end of the game, the teams congratulate each other. "Thanks for a good game," Dan says.

Now it's time for a team photo. Everyone is excited. "It's the winning team!" laughs Dan.

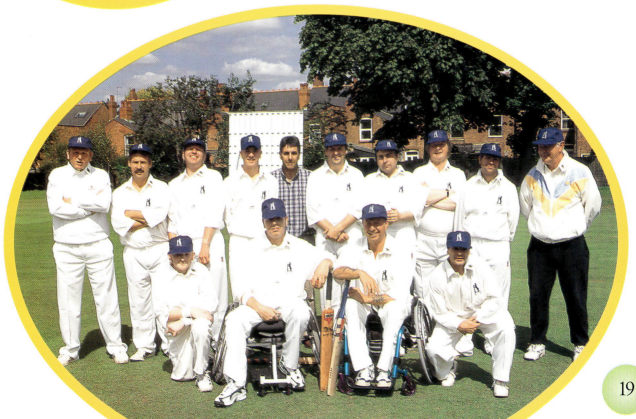

So you want to be a cricketer?

1. Join your local cricket club. There is one in most towns and villages.

2. Start practising! Cricketers need to be good at throwing and catching.

3. Cricketers need a lot of safety equipment. Most clubs have some for you to use.

4. Cricket is a summer sport. Larger clubs have indoor centres where you can practise in the nets in the winter.

5. Cricket was invented in England over a hundred years ago, Now it is played in many countries all over the world.

6. Cricket games are really long. They can last for days. So you need to have a lot of patience, too!

Facts about physical disabilities

- Physical disabilities are also called impairments. This is because a part of a person's body is impaired, or doesn't work properly.

- Some people are born with arms or legs missing, no-one knows why. False limbs or attachments help them use everyday objects or move around.

- Some people have conditions, such as cerebral palsy or muscular dystrophy, that mean they have difficulty moving parts of their bodies.

- Sometimes people injure themselves in an accident. Then they may damage part of their body. If you hurt your spine badly you may have difficulty moving parts of your body.

How you can help

- Talk directly to the disabled person. Don't talk to their companion as if they weren't there.

- Offer to help a disabled person, then wait until your offer is accepted. Find out exactly what they would like you to do.

- If you are talking to a person who is in a wheelchair, sit down so that you can look at them properly. Don't lean on a person's wheelchair.

- It's OK to use expressions such as "See you later" to a blind person or "I'll be running along now" to someone who uses a wheelchair. Don't use words such as handicapped, or spastic as disabled people find them very rude.

- Remember, you can't always see someone's disability. Speak clearly, look at the person you are speaking to – and be friendly!

Addresses and further information

RADAR - The Royal Association for Disability and Rehabilitation
12 City Forum
250 City Road
London EC1 8AF
tel. 0207 250 3222; minicom 0207 2504119;
radar@radar.org.uk; www.radar.org.uk

The Muscular Dystrophy Group
7-11 Prescott Place
London SW4 6BS

REACH National Advice Centre for Children with Reading Difficulties
Nine Mile Ride
California Country Park
Finchampstead, RG40 4HT

Muscular Dystrophy Association
Royal South Sydney Community Health Complex
Joynton Avenue, Zetland, N.S.W. 2017
Australia

Index

© 2000 Franklin Watts

Franklin Watts
96 Leonard Street
London
EC2A 4XD

Franklin Watts Australia
14 Mars Road
Lane Cove
NSW 2066

ISBN: 0 7496 3668 8

Dewey Decimal Classification
Number: 362.4

10 9 8 7 6 5 4 3 2 1

A CIP catalogue record for
this book is available from the
British Library.

Printed in Malaysia

Consultants: Sue Pratt, RADAR,
Beverley Mathias, REACH.
Editor: Samantha Armstrong
Designer: Louise Snowdon
Photographer: Chris Fairclough
Illustrator: Derek Matthews

With thanks to: Dan Holder and the
Warwickshire Disability Team.